Deliver
the Urgent Messages for America

Deliver
the Urgent Messages for America

The Urgency for U.S. Economic System Reform

Ling Ling Shi

*With tears and prayers, carried by the wings of faith and hope and love,
I am delivering the urgent messages and sharing the hope with you,
Americans and U.S. leaders.*

DELIVER THE URGENT MESSAGES FOR AMERICA
THE URGENCY FOR U.S. ECONOMIC SYSTEM REFORM

iUniverse books may be ordered through booksellers or by contacting:

iUniverse
1663 Liberty Drive
Bloomington, IN 47403
www.iuniverse.com
1-800-Authors (1-800-288-4677)

Because of the dynamic nature of the Internet, any web addresses or links contained in this book may have changed since publication and may no longer be valid. The views expressed in this work are solely those of the author and do not necessarily reflect the views of the publisher, and the publisher hereby disclaims any responsibility for them.

Unless otherwise indicated, scripture taken from the Holy Bible, NEW INTERNATIONAL VERSION®. Copyright © 1973, 1978, 1984 by Biblica, Inc. All rights reserved worldwide. Used by permission. NEW INTERNATIONAL VERSION® and NIV® are registered trademarks of Biblica, Inc. Use of either trademark for the offering of goods or services requires the prior written consent of Biblica US, Inc.

ISBN: 978-1-4917-4905-0 (sc)
ISBN: 978-1-4917-4904-3 (e)

Library of Congress Control Number: 2014920073

Printed in the United States of America.

iUniverse rev. date: 12/17/2014

This book is dedicated to our

Heavenly Father
Lord Jesus Christ
Holy Spirit

In the great desert,
Your cloud and fire led me,
In the roaring red sea,
Your almighty power made the way.

The Lord, the Lord, is my strength,
And my song, He has become my salvation.

In the journey of my life
Your love surrounds me,
In the depth of my heart and soul,
Your goodness fills me.

The Lord, the Lord, is my strength,
And my song, He has become my salvation.

This book is my sweet remembrances
and thanks to my beloved father

This book is my love and thanks
to my widowed mother

You are always in my heart

Contents

"We the People of the United States, in order to form a more perfect Union, establish Justice, insure domestic Tranquility, provide for the common defense, promote the general Welfare, and secure the Blessings of Liberty to ourselves and our Posterity, do ordain and establish this Constitution for the United States of America."

This is the opening words of the U.S. Constitution. To me, it is the U.S. Constitution Dream and the Dream for Americans. From these words, I can see that the love and faith and hope given by our loving God to His earthly children, were deeply planted in the fields of the U.S. founding fathers' souls, and flowing from within and articulating on our nation's most important document- the U.S. Constitution.

"I pledge allegiance to the Flag of the United States of America,
and to the republic for which it stands,
one Nation **under God**, indivisible,
with liberty and justice for all."

From little children to senior citizens, when we solemnly pledge to the Flag of the United States of America, we pledge to a nation with life; when we solemnly speak the words, we express our deep gratitude for this land, a land of brave and freedom and dream, we pledge our hearts of love to the people who live in this land, and to God-the Creator of the Universe.

Urgent Messages for U.S. Economic System Reform

#3 Message of Build An American ARK advocacy:

To urge the U.S. government to reform and adjust the existing economic system by establishing policies which are more fair, just, and following the free capital market principles.

#4 Message of Build An American ARK advocacy:

To establish a tax-1-2-3 simplified and transparent policy and administration system according to the Truth of God, so that individuals, families and private enterprises' tax burdens can be reduced, the existing tax procedures can be simplified, and the government operational cost can be reduced tremendously, an all win situation can be reached.

Dream

It comes from the urgent messages for U.S. economic system reform:

"Turning U.S. government tax revenues into the lakes of love and the rivers of blessing to benefit all people living in this beautiful and amazing land, a land of brave and freedom and dream, a land carried on the wings of Faith, Hope and Love, a nation built on the foundation of Christianity, by the Mercy, Forgiveness, Guidance, Grace and Love from Almighty God"

I hope and pray that the dream will come true someday—

Analysis and Advocacy for U.S. Economic System Reform

"Ask and it will be given to you, seek and you will find, knock and the door will be opened to you. For everyone who asks receives, he who seeks finds; and to him who knocks, the door will be opened" (Matthew 7:7)

Let the Word of God diagnosis U.S. economic system and give us prescription for healing.

May God's Grace and Love shine upon His children, to spring up good ideas for our nation's economic system reform.

Now,
I am going to present the messages and analysis and advocacy in Five Themes to share with you the lessons and hope that the Lord planted in my heart. May the journey in Five Themes spring up the strength within and encourage us to run a victorious race for our nation-America, the land of brave and freedom and dream!

This is the Word of God

"The fear of the LORD is the beginning of wisdom, and knowledge of the Holy One is understanding." (Proverbs 9:10)

"Unless the LORD builds the house, its builders labor in vain. Unless the LORD watches over the city, the watchmen stand guard in vain." (Psalm 127:1)

Prelude

On the Mountain of the Lord it will be provided (Genesis 22:14)

After I finished my first book *"Build An American ARK-the Strategy and Method for U.S. Economic Revival"*, my journey with Lord Jesus Christ led me to further study to find answers for how our nation could turn economic chaos to cosmos and blessing.

The Word of God revealed me the marvelous realm that the Truth of the Most High Living God-the Creator of the Universe gives the key answers.

The Truth of God-the Holy Bible, on it every U.S. President placed their hands and took oath in the U.S. President Inauguration, is an Everlasting Living Book for human lives from our Father in heaven. It established the highest Law and Decree for mankind through the histories of men's interactions with God. From Genesis to the Revelation, from cover to cover, the Holy Bible tells us-God's earthly children the Truth.

This amazing book is above all the books in the world. **All Scripture is God-breathed** (2 Timothy 3:16) and was written over the span of 1500 years by God-chosen prophets and Lord Jesus' disciples. The Holy Bible is a collection of family letters that God meant for His children to read and to abide by.

The Holy Bible covers the contents from the Faith in the Truth of God to the worldly religious, from the nature science to education, culture, politics, economy, military, medical, health, literature, arts---the Holy Bible is the comprehensive life menu for God's earthly children to walk in the Truth and to have upright meaningful lives, and to receive the Salvation of God.

Standing in the Word of God-the Truth, I want to share with Americans and U.S. leaders the urgent messages, analysis and advocacy for U.S. economic system reform through U.S. founding history, the unique role of the U.S. government and its tasks and responsibilities, the beauty in this amazing land, the hope of true recovery and revival for the U.S. economy, managing taxes revenue in wisdom, and reforming U.S. government political and economic policies in ten economy or economy-related sectors according to the Word of God.

May the Word of God and God's Love lead us to see the precious treasure, hidden treasure and hidden economic strength in America; may God's Word lead us to walk out from economic turmoil and confusion and walk into the true prosperous and blessing lives bestowed by God; may God's Word lead us to the Mountain of the Lord to receive His Goodness.

Theme I

The U.S. Constitution's revelation & The U.S. government's role

From U.S. founding history, to see who we are and what we should stand in.

The U.S. Constitution tells us: "America is a Christian nation".

Urge the U.S. government to realize that the U.S. government's role should be God's servant and people's servant.

1. The key code in the U.S. Constitution Article VII states the U.S. true identity.

In the U.S. Constitution, Article VII, it indicated: **"Done in Convention by the Unanimous Consent of the States present the Seventeenth Day of September in the Year of our Lord one thousand seven hundred and eighty seven and of the Independence of the United States of America the Twelfth in witness whereof we have hereunto subscribed our Names,"**

Including U.S. President George Washington, Benjamin Franklin, 41 U.S. founding fathers signed the U.S. Constitution Unanimously.

From this most important moment in America's history, from the Article VII, the U.S. Constitution gave us a Key Code: **"the Year of our Lord one thousand seven hundred and Eighty seven"**, a key code that tells Americans from generations to generations, to remember who America belongs to and who we are in Christ Jesus.

The key code opens our eyes to see the fact and truth that the United States of America was established in the Foundation of Christianity, the United States of America is a Christian nation, and Jesus Christ is our nation's Lord. From the key code, we should know that Christianity is not only the Faith of pilgrims, but also the Faith of the U.S. founding fathers. The key code is our nation's DNA. It enables U.S. leaders and Americans to walk out from political and religion's confusion and to know this nation's true identity. The key code seems like an endorsement on the U.S. birth certificate-the U.S. Constitution from our Lord and Savior Jesus Christ for this nation's birth and establishment.

Christianity-the U.S. founding Faith **has secured the freedom**-the gift from God to human beings in this amazing land. From religious freedom to other human rights, we experience the good characters of America's nature and practice them in every aspect of our lives. If we look around the world, we can realize that America is the nation it values freedom in most.

As it is written in 2 Corinthian 3:17 **"Where the Spirit of the Lord is, there is freedom"**, the Spirit of Christianity initiated and established the dream of freedom in America; the Spirit of Christianity enables America to stand in the world as a freedom warrior and defender.

To ensure our nation's true strength, the U.S. government should respect our nation's best character and founding Faith-the Christianity, firmly keep hold of them, and line up the government's political policies with God's Law for America rather than lowering our nation's moral standards to cater the trends of the fallen world.

2. U.S. founding fathers' faith statements.

(Quotation from "Christianity and Constitution" By John Eidsmoe, Page 12-13, 117-118)

Benjamin Franklin On June 28, 1787, 81 year-old Benjamin Franklin, the oldest delegate at the convention, delivered what was probably the most famous speech of the entire meeting. He noted that: "the small progress we have made after 4 to 5 weeks (was) melancholy proof of the imperfection of the human understanding." Rather than mere human understanding, the delegates needed something more: "the Father of lights to illuminate out understandings"! He reminded the delegates that during the war for independence they had prayed regularly to God in that very Hall: "Our prayers, Sir, were heard, and they were graciously answered." All of them could remember God's intervention on their behalf, and to that intervention they owed their victory over Great Britain. "And have we forgotten that powerful friend? Or do we imagine that we no longer need His assistance? I have lived, Sir, a long time, and the longer I live, the more convincing proofs I see of this truth-that God governs in the affairs of men. And if a sparrow cannot fall to the ground without His notice, is it probable that an empire can rise without His aid? We have been assured, Sir, in the sacred writings, that **'except the Lord build the House they labour in vain that build it'**. I firmly believe this; and I also believe that without His concurring aid we shall succeed in this political building, no better than the builders of Babel" Franklin then suggested daily prayers.

George Washington In 1787, Washington chaired the Constitutional Convention in Philadelphia, and in 1788 he was elected first President. When he took office in 1789, he established a tradition by adding to the proposed inaugural oath "So, help me, God". In addition, his inaugural address called for "fervent supplications to that Almighty Being, who rules over the universe, who presides in the councils of nations, and whose providential aids can supply every human defect," asked for "His benediction," gave "Homage to the great Author of every public and private good," declared that "every step by which (Americans) have advanced to the character of an independent nation seems to have been distinguished by some token of providential agency," warned that "the propitious smiles of Heaven can never be expected on a nation that disregards the eternal rules of order and right, which Heaven itself has ordained," and asked for the "divine blessing" of "the benign Parent of the human race".

Washington did not hesitate to declare days of prayer and thanksgiving while he was in office. The first proclamation of a national day of thanksgiving, October 3, 1789, contains ideas which provide a key to Washington's understanding of Church and State: "Whereas, it is the duty of all nations to acknowledge the Providence of Almighty God, to obey His will, to be grateful for His benefits, humbly to implore His protection and favor--- that we may then unite in most humbly offering our prayers and supplications to the great Lord and Ruler of Nations, and beseech Him to pardon our national and other transgressions; to enable us all, whether in public or private stations, to perform our several and relative duties properly and punctually; to render our national government a blessing to all the people, by constantly being a government of wise, just, and constitutional laws, discreetly and faithfully executed and obeyed; to protect and guide all sovereigns and nations (especially such as have shown kindness to us), and to bless them with good governments, peace, and concord; to promote the knowledge and practice of true religion and virtue, and the increase of science, among them and us, and, generally, to grant unto all mankind such a degree of temporal prosperity as He alone knows to be best".

From U.S. founding fathers' faith statements, we can clearly see that **Benjamin Franklin** and **George Washington** were God-chosen people and God's representatives in the U.S. government to lead this young nation, and both of them had strong faith in God.

3. The U.S. government's role according to the Word of God.

This is the Word of God in Luke 10:27, Lord Jesus said **"'Love the Lord your God with all your heart and with all your soul and with all your strength and with all your mind'; and, 'Love your neighbor as yourself.'"** This is the greatest commandment from our God to God's children and God ordained government-the U.S. government.

To U.S. government, the teaching from our Lord Jesus said in Matthews 20: 28 **"just as the Son of Man did not come to be served, but to serve"** should be the U.S. government's motto in every aspect, the Word of God should be the role definition of U.S. leaders and the U.S. government's employees. Therefore, as a Christian nation, the U.S. government's role is God's servant and people's servant.

Notes in Theme I:

1. *The United States Constitution*

2. *Christianity and the Constitution-the Faith of Our Founding Fathers Author: John Eidsmoe, Published by Baker Book House Company, www.bakeracademic.com*

Theme II

The revelation of God ordained tasks for the U.S. government

The U.S. government has God ordained identity and responsibility for serving God and serving people.

The U.S. economic system should benefit all people and for whole nation's ultimate future

1. The revelation from "the official motto-IN GOD WE TRUST" and "the portraits of our founding fathers-Benjamin Franklin and George Washington-God's representatives in the U.S. government" in U.S. dollar.

From the Word of God and an event happened in the Holy Bible-New Testament, Luke 20:22-25, let's see the one of the revelations regarding the U.S. economy:

In Luke 20:22-25: **So the spies questioned him (Jesus): "Teacher, we know that you speak and teach what is right, and that you do not show partiality but teach the way of God in accordance with the truth. Is it right for us to pay taxes to Caesar or not?" He saw through their duplicity and said to them, "Show me a denarius. Whose portrait and inscription are on it?" "Caesar's," they replied. He said to them, "Then give to Caesar what is Caesar's, and to God what is God's."**

This event and Lord's Word give us a revelation that could help us to see the relevant revelation regarding the U.S. economy through U.S. dollar.

In U.S. dollar, the official motto **"IN GOD WE TRUST"** is like "inscription". Along with it, the **"portraits of U.S. founding fathers** Benjamin Franklin & first U.S. President George Washington-God's representatives in the U.S. government" indicate that the U.S. economy should first follow God's Word, serve God's Will, and for all people's benefits. The "inscription and portraits" in U.S. dollar tell us that the U.S. government is God ordained government, neither worldly pharaoh's governments, nor worldly Caesar's governments. As a Christian nation, the U.S. government should act like born again government, speak like born again government, and fulfill the government tasks and responsibilities according to God's Will and Calling, do as it is written in the Holy Bible-the sacred book on it every U.S. President placed their hands and took oath in the U.S. President Inauguration.

2. The U.S. government should dedicate the top and best potion to God the Father, God the Son-Jesus Christ, and God the Holy Spirit by supporting God's kingdom business for people's lives and the Gospel of Salvation from generation to generation.

In the Holy Bible, the Word of God and an amazing event happened in Genesis 14: 18-20 give guidance to God ordained nation for supporting God's kingdom business with top and best portion-the 10% of the first fruit. In this historic event, our father of faith, Abraham, the first nation governed by God, with his 318 trained men defeated four kings and their armies, after victory, he received blessing and then he gave 10% to Melchizedek king of Salem-the Priest of Most High Living God.

Therefore, in America, a Christian nation, the U.S. government should contribute the top and best portion of the first fruit-the 10% of the U.S. government's revenue to God's kingdom business. One of the most important effort that the U.S. government should do for God and people is to bring back the fundamental education of the Holy Bible to the U.S. public school-K to 12 grade, so that our children and young generation could learn and experience and practice God's Word as U.S. founding fathers learned, experienced and practiced; to help our children and young generation become outstanding, humble, obedient, diligent, loving and honorable citizens, leaders, Godly fathers, mothers, daughters and sons---; let their inner natural beauty created by the Father of Heavenly Lights shine from inside to outside; let our children to have strong foundation in Truth to guide them and enable them to make right decisions in every level of their lives; to help them to know their best, meaningful lives in God's plan, and to receive the best gift of love from our Father in heaven that is a born again life in Lord Jesus Christ for every human being on earth.

If we love our children, the best love we should give to them is caring their soul's health and wealth; the best love we should give to them is giving them all kinds of chances to know who they are in our Lord and Savior Christ Jesus.

To the U.S. government who governs a nation built on the foundation of Christianity, its main characters should be an honorable, humble, obedient and faithful servant for God and people; its main responsibilities and tasks should be leading and helping people living in this land to know God, promoting upright lifestyle according to the Truth, working with Churches of Jesus Christ in harmonies and side by side and hand in hand, providing best chance and environment to bring people to God as Churches of Jesus Christ do, and leading entire nation to try best to fulfill the U.S. Constitution Dream.

The fundamental teaching of the Holy Bible in the public school is so important from generation to generation. It is our lifeline. I believe that if the U.S. government can take this issue seriously, we will see that the criminal rate dropping, the prisons closing one by one, the rehabilitation center getting empty, ---all negative things happening in our young generation and entire nation will be turned to hope, their lives will shine, they will be able to become the salt of the earth and light of the world, their lives will be blessed, their families will be blessed, their community will be blessed and our nation will be blessed truly and indeed.

How beautiful it is for us to see our children live in the light and please God as it is written in 3 John 1:4 **"I have no greater joy than to hear that my children are walking in the truth."** This is our Father's voice and Will, this is His great Love to all His children on earth.

"God is Love", and **"Love never failed."** If we are willing to walk with God humbly, His Love will hold our children in His Loving Palms and carry us to His promised land. Lord Jesus said in Matthew 19:14 **"Let the little children come to me, and do not hinder them, for the kingdom of heaven belongs to such as these."**

Economy is important for a nation, but, the Spiritual teaching and guidance in the Word of God is more important, for the Word of God said in Matthew 4:4 **"Man does not live on bread alone, but on every word that comes from the mouth of God".** To apply God's Word in the U.S. economy and the modern world, I can realize that "a nation does not live on its GDP, but on every words that comes from the mouth of God".

3. From the U.S. Constitution opening words, to recall the American dream and the calling for the U.S. government from God.

The U.S. Constitution, done in Convention by the Unanimous Consent of the States present <u>the Seventeenth Day of September in</u> **the Year of our Lord** <u>one thousand seven hundred and Eighty seven</u> and of the Independence of the United States of America, is the supreme law of the United States of America.

From its opening words:

"We the People of the United States, in order to form a more perfect Union, establish Justice, insure domestic Tranquility, provide for the common defense, promote the general Welfare, and secure the Blessings of Liberty to ourselves and our Posterity, do ordain and establish this Constitution for the United States of America."

We see a beautiful blue print and dream for the people living in this amazing land; we see that the U.S. government's tasks and responsibilities were ordained by God to fulfill His Will for His children; we see that God is the Author for the American dream, a beautiful dream on earth for human beings in the midst of crooked and depraved world and generations.

God is Justice and righteousness, full of Mercy and Compassion for all His people. As a nation ordained by God, U.S. economic system must be established in the foundation of justice and loving mercy. It should not favor on any giant or interest group, but for all people's benefits and for whole nation's ultimate future.

If the U.S. economic system could be built on pure foundation-the Truth of God, the forces of corruption will have no power to endanger our nation's future, and by the Power and Blessing of Most High Living God, the U.S. Constitution Dream will come true and stand firmly.

Theme III

Unveiling and sharing the wisdom from Word of God for the U.S. economy and the urgency for U.S economic system reform.

God's Word in the Holy Bible reveals the way how our nation can keep a true free capital market and give people freedom and free will to practice individual dream and its fulfillment, how the U.S. government can set up economy and economy-related policies in justice and how the U.S. government can solve its financial deficits and debts.

Sharing the ideas based on the Word of God for the dream of "turning the U.S. government taxes revenue into the lakes of love and the rivers of blessing to benefit all people living in this beautiful and amazing land, a land of brave and freedom and dream, a land carried on the wings of Faith, Hope and Love, a nation built on the foundation of Christianity, by the Mercy, Forgiveness, Guidance, Grace and Love from Almighty God" in ten economy and economy-related sectors.

1. The revelation from taxpayers' money-the people's wealth and saving

First, I want to share with Americans and U.S. leaders **the strength and hope from taxpayers' money-the U.S. government tax revenues**. From this point, we will sail into an amazing channel linking to the springs of love and rivers of blessing.

The brief information or data regarding the U.S. government yearly tax revenues, expenditures in medical and social security and other useful data related to the U.S. economy which will be used in a series of analysis are listed in spreadsheet-1.

Basically, the majority of the U.S. government revenues comes from the U.S. government yearly tax revenues including payroll tax, income tax, property tax, sales tax, import tax, estates tax and gift tax, as well as various fees.

---Spreadsheet-1 (Basic Data for comparison and analysis):

BASIC DATA (WILL BE USED IN A SERIES OF ANALYSIS)	AMOUNT (APPROXIMATELY)
Total 2012 Tax Revenue	$2.45 trillion = $2,450,000,000,000
2012 Payroll Tax Revenue for Social Security & Medical	$1.377 trillion = $1,377,000,000,000
2012 Social Security & Medical Expenditure	$1.359 trillion = $1,359,000,000,000
Total U.S. incorporated City	35000 Cities in the U.S.
Total U.S. County	3144 Counties in the U.S.
The U.S. Population	316,128,839
The U.S. Families/Household	112,000,000
Elder (age 65 and older)	43,309,650
Total Hospital in the U.S.	6,411
Total Hospital Employees	5,174,262
Total Hospital Annual Payroll	$197,153,694,000
Total Clinic in the U.S.	69,342
Total Clinic Annual Payroll	$58,974,490,000
Total Clinic Employees:	2,830,582
The U.S. government gross public debts at the end of Dec. 2013	$17.226 trillion = $17,226,000,000,000
The U.S. government public debts owe in Social Security at the end of Dec. 2013	$2.7 trillion = $2,700,000,000,000
The U.S. government deficit in 2013	$680 billion = $680,000,000,000
18 to 24 years old young Americans	31,000,000
People who are held by justice system (year 2006's number):	7,200,000
Unemployed people	12,000,000
The U.S. Public School from K-12	98,817
0-5 years old children	24,000,000
The U.S. government financial bailouts in 2008	$700 billion = $700,000,000,000

Now, I am going to analyze how tax revenues derived only from **"one year payroll tax" is plentiful and more than enough to build or create what people need.** I will make two different assumptions.

(After the hospitals or clinics are built according to my analysis below in two different assumption, how can we operate and maintain these medical facilities healthily, positively and effectively in long term? The method and strategy regarding these issues will not be discussed here in detail, please refer to my book "Build An American ARK-the Strategy and Method for U.S. Economic Revival".)

1. First assumption: using 100% of **one year payroll tax revenue** to create what we need for "National Medical & Health Care System" or for "Free Decent Senior Living Community".

---Spreadsheet-2:

IF TOTAL PAYROLL TAX REVENUES $1,377,000,000,000 IN 2012 BE USED TO BUILD/CREATE:	THEN, WE CAN BUILD/CREATE
City Clinic (at cost $1 million / facility)	1,377,000 Clinics in the U.S.
County Hospital (at cost $100 million/ facility)	13,770 Hospitals in U.S.
Senior free decent apartment for elder-age 65 and older (at cost $30,000 per unit)	45,900,000 Senior Apartments in the U.S.

MATH CALCULATION	HOW MANY FACILITIES WE CAN BUILD IN EACH U.S. CITY OR COUNTY?
$1,377,000,000,000 ÷ $1,000,000 = 1,377,000 Clinics	1,377,000 ÷ 35,000 = about 39 clinics /city
$1,377,000,000,000 ÷ $100,000,000 = 13,770 Hospitals	13,770 ÷ 3,144 = about 4 hospitals/county
$1,377,000,000,000 ÷ $30,000 = 45,900,000 units senior free decent apartment	45,900,000 ÷ 35,000 = about 1311 Apt units/city

2. Second assumption: using 50% of one year payroll tax revenues to create what we need for "National Medical & Health Care System" or for "Free Decent Senior Living Community", and another 50% continues to be used in the U.S. government's current way through insurance programs etc and working with service providers in private sectors to handle people's medical and retirement needs.

---Spreadsheet-3:

IF 50% OF TOTAL PAYROLL TAX REVENUES $1,377,000,000,000 IN 2012 BE USED TO BUILD/CREATE:	THEN, WE CAN BUILD/CREATE
City Clinic (at cost $1 million /facility)	688,500 Clinics in the U.S.
County Hospital (at cost $100 million/facility)	6,885 Hospitals in U.S.
Senior free decent apartment for elder-age 65 and older (at cost $30,000 per unit)	22,950,000 Senior Apartments in the U.S.

MATH CALCULATION	HOW MANY FACILITIES WE CAN BUILD IN EACH U.S. CITY OR COUNTY?
$1,377,000,000,000÷2 = $688,500,000,000 $688,500,000,000 ÷ $1,000,000 = 688,500 Clinics	688,500÷ 35,000 = about 20 clinics /city
$1,377,000,000,000÷2 = $688,500,000,000 $688,500,000,000 ÷ $100,000,000 = 6,885 Hospitals	6,885÷3,144 = about 2 hospitals/county
$1,377,000,000,000÷2 = $688,500,000,000 $688,500,000,000÷ $30,000 = 22,950,000 units senior free decent apartment	22,950,000÷35,000 = about 655 Apt units/city

So, from the above simple analysis based on first assumptions in spreedsheet-2, we can see that only using **"one year payroll tax revenue"**, we can build hospitals and clinics nationwide **more than** what U.S. has now to meet whole nation's Medical & Healthcare needs (Refer to the statistical data in Spreadsheet-1), and more than 8 million people could have new job opportunities. With ongoing hard work and management in Godly wisdom, soon or later, we will reach the realm of no more jobless, no more lacking, no more sorrow, and no more helpless---, it is full of hope in the Love of God!

In the same way, from the above simple analysis based on first assumption in spreedsheet-2, we can see that only using **one year payroll tax revenue**, we can build senior decent apartments or retirement communities for all elders, our parents and the generations to come. How hopeful and joyful it is!

From the second assumption in spreedsheet-3, we can see that with only **50% of one year payroll tax revenues**, we still have satisfactory results to let "National Medical & Health Care" dream comes true as well as to provide all elders free decent senior communities and to enable them to enjoy worry free retirement lives.

So, the revelation from above simple analysis is that: in America, **we have strong ability and more than enough financial resources to build and create what people need in "National Medical & Health Care" and "Social Security Related Long Term Benefits" by people's own money- the U.S. government's tax revenues.**

The revelation from above simple analysis tells us that **if** the U.S. government can handle taxpayers' money correctly and manage it **in active approach** to create and build what we need, the people in the U.S. will be free from the worry of medical and health care needs, be free from the worry of elders living burdens, be free from the worry for many and many things. The analysis and its revelation tells us that a good system will enable all people in America to dream the dream of love for our families, our communities and societies, our churches, our nation and the world!

In addition, the revelation from the above simple analysis also tells us that the tax burdens to everyone, every family and every private business could be reduced tremendously, **because we don't need too much for the U.S. government to accomplish its responsibilities and tasks if U.S. government could manage taxpayers' money-people's wealth and saving in active approaches, act and work with mentality and methods of creation.**

However, what have we seen and experienced in reality?

The reality in the U.S. is totally different than what I discovered and presented in the above simple analysis. The reality is that the U.S. government has suffered deficits and debts over decades, the deficits and debts surpass what Americans can bear, the tax burdens to people and private enterprises keep growing and growing, and the U.S. government is always in shortage. **Why?**

Through my prayer and study, I have found that the Word of God can give us answers and solutions, and the Word of God can lead us to discover the serious mistakes in U.S. government taxes collection and revenues' operation and management.

Thanks to God, His promise in Jeramiah 33:3 for His earthly children can comfort us and encourage us, and gives us assurance of the U.S. economy system reform and healing: **"Call to me and I will answer you and tell you great and unsearchable things you do not know"**. I believe that as long as Americans and the U.S. government take the present situation seriously and humbly come to God and ask God's intervene as U.S. founding fathers did, we will be able to walk out from economic turmoil, and taste the living water of God from every aspects of our nation's life.

Now, let's first take look of the urgency for U.S. debts and deficits, then let Word of God tells us the answers, and open our eyes to see where the solution is.

2. The U.S. government debts and deficits and the urgency for our nation.

From the following analysis in spreadsheet-4, let's see how urgent it is to reform the U.S. government economy policies and the way of taxes collection and revenues' operation and management:

---Spreadsheet-4:

THE U.S. GOVERNMENT GROSS PUBLIC DEBTS AT THE END OF DEC. 2013	IF DISTRIBUTING THESE HUGE DEBTS TO EACH INDIVIDUAL IN THE U.S., WHAT DOES THAT MEAN?
$17.226 trillion	Each individual in the U.S. owes $54,616 debt

THE U.S. GOVERNMENT PUBLIC DEBTS OWE IN SOCIAL SECURITY AT THE END OF DEC. 2013	WHAT THAT MEANS?
$2.7 trillion = $2,700,000,000,000	It means about 2 years social security and medical expenditure reserve have been spent by the U.S. government

MATH CALCULATION	MORE DANGERS COME FROM THE U.S. GOVERNMENT DEFICITS:
$17,226,000,000,000÷ 316,128,839 = $54,616 debt each individual in the U.S. (based on population of 316,128,839)	$680 billion deficit in 2013, It means that the debts owed by each individual in the U.S. has increased $2,151 in 2013

MATH CALCULATION	MORE DANGERS COME FROM THE U.S. GOVERNMENT DEFICITS:
$2,700,000,000,000÷ $1,359,000,000,000 = about 2 years	The U.S. government deficit in 2013 has swallowed 680,000 new city clinics (at 1 million cost) or 6,800 new county hospitals (at 100 million cost)

From the above data and simple analysis in spreadsheet-4, we can see the dangers that threaten our nation's future.

The revelation from the above analysis tells us that the hope for U.S. economic true recovery and revival is in our land and it waits for us to wake up and to re-think, but in the meantime, the dangers are crouching at our doors and threat America's today and tomorrow.

Dear Americans and U.S. leaders, to face the reality, we have to take the situation seriously to respond the urgency without delay. If we do so with responsibility, humble, hard work, freedom, faith, hope and love, we will defeat the dangers, reform the U.S. economy system according to the Truth and walk into the realm of God's Blessing and Heavenly prosperity. For God gives us His Promise for His earthly children in Genesis 22:14 **«On the mountain of the LORD it will be provided.»** Let's climb the Mountain of the Lord with the heart of **"Love your neighbor as yourself"** to find solution.

3. From God's Word in the Holy Bible, to discover the powerful economic principles in modern economic system and the formation of the U.S. government debts and economic crises.

God is the Creator of the Universe, He created the natural world and spiritual world. God created Laws for both realms. He often uses natural Law to lead human beings' understanding in His spiritual Law, uses natural condition and phenomena to reveal our spiritual condition and crisis, and use spiritual Law and revelation to reveal our natural condition and crisis. If we respect God's Word and deeply study His Word in the Holy Bible, we will gain Godly wisdom to run victorious lives.

Now, let me share with you the Word of God and answer the questions and thinking above:

This is the Word of God in Leviticus 19:19:

"'Keep my decrees. 'Do not mate different kinds of animals. 'Do not

plant your field with two kinds of seed. 'Do not wear clothing woven of two kinds of material.'"

This is the Word of God in Deuteronomy 22:10:

"Do not plow with an ox and a donkey yoked together"

The Word of God gives us the fundamental and key economic principle for our nation, as well as for the world:

From the Scripture and God's decree: **"Do not mate different kinds of animals"**, I can understand that the U.S. government **cannot** mate with private businesses to become clone entities to operate and manage taxpayers' money, and to fulfill government tasks or responsibilities for all people.

Applying the Word of God to our nation's economic environment, I can understand that the U.S. government is an entity who is appointed to work in the people's field to take care of the field and raise harvest for all Americans' interest and future, to fulfill the U.S. Constitution Dream for all. But, private businesses are the entities who are motivated to make money, gain profit for their owners or shareholders, and working in their own private fields or free capital market.

If I call these two kinds entities are two kinds of animals, they are not created for same purpose, they are totally different animal and they are different in nature. They **cannot** be mated or be cloned to become clone entity. If we do clone, the animal from clone will be an unhealthy animal and it will easily get sick and die.

From the Scripture and God's decree: **"Do not plant your field with two kinds of seed"**, I can understand that the seed in the U.S. government's hand is the taxpayers' money-people's wealth and saving, the seed in private business giants or any size businesses is the seed of their private investments. These two kinds of seed bear different motivation and purpose, so, they **cannot** be mixed to plant on same field.

From the Scripture and God's decree: **"Do not wear clothing woven of two kinds of material"**, I can understand that the U.S. government wears a cloth and its fabric shall be only made by the thread of "responsible for all people", but, private businesses entities wear clothes with the fabrics, in most time, made by the thread of "responsible for business owners or shareholders". Two kinds of threads cannot mixed together and to weave or spin to make clothes for both.

From the Scripture and God's decree: **"Do not plow with an ox and a donkey yoked together"**, I can understand that if I analogy a donkey as the U.S. government, and an ox as private businesses entities, they **cannot** be yoked together and plow same filed.

Unfortunately, the U.S. government economy policies and system just stand in opposite, contrary with the Word of God and the basic economy principle revealed by Word of God. For example, the **"Federal Reserve System"** is a financial clone system, owned by private bankers or banking giants, but has authority from the U.S. Congress to operate and manage the U.S. government tax revenues-the people's money, to make and control economic policies, as well as to dominate the U.S. and worldly economic system and environment. Its formation, function and operation are totally contrary with the Word of God from the beginning of its establishment.

The U.S. government's purpose and function are different than private businesses. The government's tasks should be managing people's money and wealth for all people's interests with "**risk free management method**"; the government's motivation **should be taking care of** all levels of people. In contrast, private businesses' motivation is mostly personal financial gains or personal dream fulfillment, driven by maximize profit for their own. Of course, there are hundreds and thousands private businesses are heartfelt to serve people, help people and communities.

The clone entities between the U.S. government and private businesses, as well as the U.S. government economic policies and system which favor the interest groups and private business giants or entities have broken the free capital market principles, they have made the free capital market not truly free, and caused free capital market seriously sick.

The Word of God and the history of economic crises have given America urgent calls to re-examine the U.S. government economic policies and system, as well as to have urgency of reform.

Now, I am going to share my studies, and ideas planted and guided by the Word of God and His teaching in ten economy and economy-related sectors based on the #3 & #4 messages of "Build An American ARK" Advocacy.

May the dream of **"Turning U.S. government tax revenues into the lakes of love and the rivers of blessing to benefit all people living in this beautiful and amazing land, a land of brave and freedom and dream, a land carried on the wings of Faith, Hope and Love, a nation built on the foundation of Christianity, by the Mercy, Forgiveness, Guidance, Grace and Love from almighty God"** come true.

4. Sharing the ideas in ten economy and economy-related sectors:

This is Word of God in Matthew 9:16-17: **"No one sews a patch of unshrunk cloth on an old garment, for the patch will pull away from the garment, making the tear worse. Neither do men pour new wine into old wineskins. If they do, the skins will burst, the wine will run out and the wineskins will be ruined. No, they pour new wine into new wineskins, and both are preserved."**

Basically, I advocate the U.S. government to form a Non-Profit Industries and Services Organization Group contributed by the U.S. government tax revenues-taxpayers' money-people's wealth and saving, and to serve people and for all people's interests besides current government management system, to enter into the free capital market, to follow free capital market principle, to create and build what people need in active, diligent, and effective way with long term vision to fulfill the U.S. government's tasks and responsibilities ordained by God in this Christian nation.

(The detail discussion for the Non-Profit Industries and Services Organization Group, please refer to my book "Build An American ARK-the Strategy and Method for U.S. Economic Revival)

In the meantime, I advocate the U.S. government to simplify its current operation and management system, to reduce the size, to cut government's expenditures, to strive maximizing the U.S. government's function to serve people with responsibility, humble, diligent and love, to release the tax burdens from people and business entities, to be able to pay the U.S. government debts and reduce the deficits through hard work, thrifty, government-discipline and creative approach, to secure the environment in this amazing land to let people enjoy true freedom, peace and abound lives in God the Father, God the Son-Jesus Christ,and God the Holy Spirit.

Now, let me share the ideas of economic reform in ten economy and economy-related sectors:

Banking and Financing system

Keeping taxpayers' money and wealth safe, secure and creative.

(1) **Establishing the "Lake of Tax Revenues" which is a safe, secured and real "Central Banking System" to manage and operate tax revenues.**

The fundamental and key principle previously discussed based on the Word of God has clear indication and guidance for the separation between taxpayers' money and private financial giants, and it is very important. The U.S. government should consider to establish a real "Central Banking System" within 50 states, contributed by people, owned by people, worked for people, and under the U.S. government management and operation to fulfill the U.S. government's tasks and responsibilities for all.

Dear Americans and U.S. leaders, The Word of God is Life, it is written in Matthew 24: 35 **"Heaven and earth will pass away, but my words will never pass away"**, from individuals to families, from families to communities, from communities to nation, we need study God's Word, obey God's Word, and to be equipped to confront crisis and storm from every aspect. If we prepare well, when the day of crisis and storm come, we may be able to stand firm and be steadfast.

If people's money can be secured and preserved in a "lake of tax revenues" with a management and operation system in Godly wisdom and in justice for all people's interests, with the mind set of minimizing the risks and maximizing the tax revenues' function for everyone's needs, not only that the U.S. government yearly tax rates can be reduced tremendously, but also, with the heart of **"love your neighbor as yourself"**, the "lake of tax revenues" will become the "lakes of love" and the "rivers of blessing" to all.

(2) Setting up strict regulation and laws for those private businesses who involve in the U.S. government's programs under present system

The U.S. government should set up laws to regulate wages, benefits, bonus, compensations, shareholders profits, and dividends for those businesses who are handling the U.S. government tax revenues or investments or receiving government's bailouts.

As long as private businesses receive the U.S. government contracts or involve in the U.S. government programs or touch people's money, their businesses conducts should be checked by the U.S. government and people in order to make "Commercial and Government Entity" system transparent, prevent power abusing or money abusing, protect people's interests, ensure the lake is safe and without leaking.

In Banking and Financing Market System, the following vital areas are worthy for Americans and U.S. leaders to think:

(1) Credit System's nature, function, power and abusing.

(2) Credit System's application and its effect to people's freedom and rights.

(3) Insurance System's nature, function, power and abusing.

(4) Unfair and unjust wealth re-distribution through Insurance System.

(5)   How to prevent the dangerous "privatization of people's wealth" when we face economic crises in current economic system.

National Medical & Health Care System

Establishing National Medical & Health Care System to benefit all people and all entities through creation in active approach.

(1)   **Using tax revenues to build hospitals and clinics, and to establish National Medical & Health Care System with long term vision**

Financial market in private sector is high risky market, **the major form of risky market is "insurance industry".**

The U.S. government should prevent to put and invest payroll tax revenues in such risky market. Social Security Funds should become working capital and be invested to establish tangible assets and long term operational facilities to create what people need rather than invest "Funds" to private financial investment market.

"Insurance Program" should only exist in private market, not for the U.S. government to use and play. Depends on "Insurance Program" will cause us to face unceasing soaring cost for medical and health care.

With the frequent occurrence of natural disasters, the rise of terrorist and moral corruption etc, the insurance industry will face the challenges like never before. **So, the U.S. government needs new era's strategy and method besides insurance industry to fulfill government's tasks and responsibilities.**

The analysis in the spreadsheet 2 & 3 gives us a positive vision of building and creating enough city clinics, county hospitals nationwide by payroll tax revenue. In addition, establishing pharmaceutical factories and setting up pharmacies inside clinics and hospitals are also important and effective for reducing overall cost in Medical and Health Care System.

I believe that by faith, hope and love, with hard work, diligent, thrifty mind, honor, and humble, the dream of National Medical and Health Care System will come true.

(2) Re-evaluate and examine the cost and charges in hospitals and clinics with government contracting for Medicare and Medicaid under present system

To prevent overcharges, system complication and wasting, to reduce government's burdens and people's burden, setting up a transparent "Simplified Medical Operation and Management System" is important. To discipline medical and health care industries and to promote working ethic with love and honor in such industries are necessary, especially in a Christian nation. Tolerating the unceasing soaring on medical cost and depending on insurance industry will lead our nation running closer and closer to the dangerous cliff.

Since America was built on the foundation of Christianity, we still can see and experience some upright characters under present medical and health care system. For instance, the charity care programs in private hospitals are very friendly and good public services and contribution, they are the manifestation of social virtue in our nation. Those impressive programs filled with compassion and mercy and love under present private medical and health care sector should become exemplary programs for medical system and be promoted.

It is possible in America to have a peaceful coexistence and a win-win medical system between taxpayers owned hospitals and clinics and private medical providers who have government contracting **if** we honor and follow God's Commandment-**"Love your neighbor as yourself"**.

In Medical & Health Care System, the following issues are worthy for Americans and U.S. leaders to think:

(1) The consequences of the current spoiled medical & health care system and the U.S. government's responsibilities for the spoiled market.

(2) The long-term vision/sight for "co-existence" of private medical Industry and National Medical & Health Care System, and its benefits to all people.

(3)   Extend the scope for non-prescription medicine.

(4)   Solving an issue seriously for Medicaid patients' waiting and appointment time, and to ensure the elders or patients who are under government Medicaid program could receive services from private medical providers without ridiculous and incredible waiting time.

Social Security System

Making the "Social Security System" real "Secure" for all through creation in active approach.

The U.S. government needs to change its investment strategy from putting "Funds" in various private financial market products into creating tangible industries, not only for the National Medical & Health Care System, but also in taking care the responsibilities for the following:

(1)   For retirements and all Elders and Widows

Using part of FICA-OASDI fund to build "Senior Decent Free Apartment/ Community" combined with the National Medical & Health Care System discussed before, to provide full living supports and services for all elders. Setting up different levels of living supports for all elders in accordance with different abilities and needs.

For widows, if they do not reach age 65 but they have needs for house to live, the U.S. government should give them privilege to receive living supports same as elders without waiting period.

The analysis in spreadsheet 2 & 3 shows us the positive vision. By active approach and creative mind set, it is possible that all elders and widows could enjoy their lives with blessing and be worry free.

(2)   For Poor and Poor Family

To give long term and positive helping to the poor and poor families, the U.S. government needs create job opportunities to those who are living on welfares. Helping them to build up the confidence in job market by supporting them in education, career training and skill training, providing children caring and enable parents to work, giving them chances to work in public sectors, encouraging them walk out from passive mind set and environment and overcome difficulties which kept them living on welfare, supporting them in food, house, education and medical & health care in exchange with their certain work in public sectors.

Using part of Social Security Fund to create job opportunities specifically for poor and poor families.

(3) For Orphan and Abused Children

To build **"Children Living Garden Network"** -a full living care communities for orphans and abused children and help them grow up with a upright lives; to encourage the people who have loving hearts to become their Godly parents by involving children rescuing and cultivation programs within the children living garden network.

Examining current foster family law and prevent unreasonable allocation and wasting on government funds; to prevent those children be destroyed by human trafficking, take care of them until they find decent careers or jobs, with no age 16 limitation; protecting those children's basic human rights in adoption according to God's Law and Will when they under 16 years old and have no ability to make right choice for their own; to evaluate adoption families' qualification according to God's Law and Will.

Providing complete supports and protections for those unfortunate children before they grow up is the U.S. government's undeniable responsibilities and charity tasks ordained by God. God is the Father of fatherless, He cares every single child's life.

May orphans and abused children enjoy their lives without sorrow, burden and helpless in this Christian nation; may orphans and abused children be blessed in this Christian nation.

(4) For the Disabled

Providing complete basic living supports without time limitation to those who disable to work due to birth defect or different kinds of injury or sickness. Turning "Disability Insurance Funds" from risky financial market investment into a creative and healthy system which could run by itself in long term, such as building long term living support facilities or business entities. Within the system, create job opportunities for those who are recovered or partially recovered from injuries or sickness back to work based on their physical condition and abilities.

(5) For Veteran and Family

The U.S. government should provide complete life supports for veteran and secure their jobs unconditionally. Especially to those families they lost their loved one in war, the U.S. government should take care of their families unconditionally, from job to education, from house to food---, comfort them and encouragement them for their sacrifice to defend the freedom and peace.

The U.S. government should also investment related funds with active approach to create job opportunities inside the U.S. Military. This topic will continue be discussed in the section of "War & Homeland Security"

In Social Security System, the following issues are worthy for Americans and U.S. leaders to think:

(1) The dangerous tunnels and sinks of re-distribution of people's wealth and saving-the tax revenues.

(2) The risky investment methods and ways on the "Funds of Social Security System", and the favor to capitalists.

(3) The facts to cause polarization between rich and poor and the U.S. government's responsibility for the existing polarization; the U.S. government's tasks to take care of the poor or weak or despised or lower or unfortunate people in this Christian nation.

(4) How can the U.S. government keep the capitalism system and at the same time, do justly and love mercy to all people? How to make existing capitalism system running in healthy under God's Law? What are the capitalism's positive nature and negative nature?

(5) Re-evaluating and examining private business providers with government contracting in present time and under present system, and to ensure the system running in justice and fairness.

Employment and Unemployment

Enhancing the health of employment market and system. To reform the U.S. labor law for protecting jobless people's rights. Extinguishing nationwide unemployment.

The U.S. government should stand in the Truth of God to defend upright moral and ethics in workplace. The corruption of job market moral and ethics will directly affect whole nation's moral standard and living environment and quality and tranquility. Tolerating corruption and political darkness in workplace will make more and more people depressed and oppressed. There are many critical issues in job market and workplaces need the U.S. government to take action to reform labor law.

(1) **Protecting all workers' rights and taking government's responsibility to set up just law and system for all employees and employers**

Employees who currently belong to "bargaining unit" (union members) or employees who are "individuals" should have equal rights and opportunities to receive the protection from "Just Labor Law and System".

To protect job market's fairness and justice between all employees and employers in America is the U.S. government's undeniable duties. The U.S. Judicial system should involve this area seriously and directly rather than leave it to private organization or entity, such as unions. To establish a simplified, instant, straight and effective system of appeal and mediation and arbitration by the U.S. government from federal to states in each county is very important.

(2) **Protecting employees who suffer unlawful orders from employers with fast and effective appeal system in each county for them to submit their grievance.**

These kinds of pressures in working place for employees are critical. The U.S. government needs to set up fast appeal system to protect employees' rights to do right and lawful things without job loss threaten or retaliation from employers.

(3) **Protecting employees who are facing unfair laid off or fire due to refuse obeying the wrong orders or commands from their employers.**

To protect the oppressed employees who are facing unlawful or unfair laid off or fire, the U.S. government should set up fast appeal system to stop employers' unlawful or unfair decision and to maintain employees' job and payroll from employers without loss or be turned to government's UI program-the unemployment insurance.

(4) **Establishing efficient and practical protection and arbitration system for people who lost Job to accept and handle their post-grievance.**

To establish appeal system to accept, review and make judgment for unemployed workers' cases to make sure the laid off or fire are lawful, to take their grievance seriously. To reform the labor law to give better protection for jobless families by ongoing payroll supplement from former employers. Reform labor law with justice and loving mercy.

(5) **Reform current "UI" system's policies and procedure to protect employees rights. For long term purpose, establish creative and re-creative industries to replace "UI" system.**

First, "UI" is insurance system, "UI" should be responsible for all employees who lost job either be laid off or fired unconditionally; Employers should not have any rights to protest employees to apply UI after they lost job; To all people who lost job no matter what reasons behind are subject to receive "UI" without condition or interview or excuse. The timing for people who lost job to receive UI to partially cover their financial loss is so critical.

Second, "UI" system is an insurance system, it is not strong and healthy to handle unemployment. For long term purpose, the U.S. government should change "UI-Funds" into creation, to provide more job opportunities to absorb joblessness and strengthen the job market directly.

Finally, **"Love your neighbor as yourself"** will bring our leaders to jobless people's shoes to think more and to bring real effective plan into job market and to extinguish our nation's high unemployment.

The goal to changing "UI" into creative and re-creative industries could be reached when you link "UI" with other nine economy or economy-related sectors. The answer could be found there.

(For extinguishing unemployment nationwide, please refer to my book "Build An American ARK-the Strategy and Method for U.S. Economic Revival)

(6) Reform labor law regarding "severance pay".

"Severance Pay" shall be mandated by law for employers to pay employees who are laid off or fired; it shall also be protected by law for every employee who lost job to take legal action against employers without losing severance pay.

"Severance Pay" should not be involved with "employment termination/ separation agreement"; The U.S. government should reform labor law to prohibit employers by any means to deprive employees legal rights, to take employees advantage, to silence employees by paying severance with certain condition, such as giving up legal action; The U.S. government should protect all employees who are facing job loss to have chance to speak the truth and submit their grievances in the U.S. courts. Let justice speaks for the oppressed one.

(7) Reform labor law regarding "employers' violation"

The U.S. labor law should set up "immediate action requirement" without complicated appeal procedures for employees to be compensated in the case of employers' violation.

Protecting employees' rights, their lives and their families lives not be jeopardized by laid off or fire is the U.S. government's responsibility. The U.S. government's obligation is not finished or ended in "UI" system for people who are suffering jobless.

(8) Reform labor law to protect employees' religious rights

Setting up labor law to protect employees' job and rights for those who choose to attend Church or religious activity or keep the Sabbath day holy for worshipping God in Saturday and Sunday.

In Employment and Unemployment issues, the following vital areas are worthy for Americans and U.S. leaders to think:

(1)   The negative impact of high unemployment to a nation's tranquility.

(2)   Negative effects on people's health caused by unemployment.

(3)   What are humble and servant minded government and its system and structure?

(4)   Union system's positive and negative nature, power, and authority.

(5)   Unions' "collective bargaining agreement" and discrimination issues.

(6)   Unions' membership policies and critical issues vs. human being free will and rights.

(7)   The justice issues on the legislation for unions' power and authority.

(8)   As a Christian nation, how to apply God's Word "Love your neighbor as yourself" in workplace?

(9)   The U.S. government's responsibilities and obligations for those who committed crimes and suffer jobless. Does it urgent for the U.S. education system reform according to the Truth of God?

(10) What is the real second chance for those who committed crimes and suffer jobless? How does it affect domestic tranquility?

National Education System

Turning U.S. national education system into a healthy and blessing system for our young generation.

(1)   **The missing of teaching and respecting for the Word of God in the U.S. public school system has raised bitter fruits to our young generation's life and caused whole nation, from individuals to families, and from communities to government**

suffering the consequences of education system's confusion and deviation.

This is the God's Word in the Holy Bible Genesis 1:1 "In the beginning God created the heavens and the earth." In the past decades, in this Christian nation, the Word of God-the Holy Bible has been moved out from our public school education system, instead, Darwin's theory of evolution which totally against the Truth of God has been promoted in school system, and it has dominated our young generation's minds, and unfairly forfeited children's rights to know the Truth of life. Moreover, many upside down political policies are forcefully entered the U.S. public school system and they are not only weakening the U.S. public school education function and twisting U.S. public school ultimate purpose, but also endangering entire nation's today and tomorrow.

(2) Let founding father George Washington and Benjamin Franklin become role models of our children

Leading our young generation to learn from U.S. founding fathers who were fear the Lord and had upright and honored lives, such as George Washington and Benjamin Franklin, will bless our nation and our children from generation to generation. To keep U.S. founding fathers' lights on and to carry on their legacy of faith, hope and love in Lord Jesus Christ will make the U.S. education system shine in the fallen world.

(3) The true love and freedom to our children

The true love and freedom giving to our children is to lead them to the Truth of God-the Word of God, there is no greater love than loving our children's soul. In education system, it is important than anything that to make sure our children's souls are in safe, secure, and protected by God. To bring back the Holy Bible teaching in the U.S. public school from K-12 grade is vital, it matters our country's future.

(4) Let our children inherit the legacy of prayer in school and experience the Power of God for their lives

God created us, He know how to bring His earthly children to true blessing. Pray to God freely in school is children's basic rights; it is also our nation's legacy and most valuable memory and beauty in the U.S. education system. Giving this precious right back to our young generation is U.S. government's responsibility to God and to people in this Christian nation. God Himself will protect and bless our education system if the U.S. government humbly to seek and obey God's Law.

(5) Let our children from "preschool to 12 grade" to enjoy more education aid

If the U.S. government can management tax revenues in Godly wisdom, a burden free education system which not only provide free education, but also can provide extended caring after school normal hours, will come true. Please see the assumption and analysis in spreadsheet 5 & 6.

To provide our children with good education and to reduce parents' burdens by additional education aid are much important then bailout bankers. I am going to use the same number of 700 billion which was used as bailouts in the 2008 economy crisis, to show Americans and U.S. leaders, how good it is for the U.S. government invests money in correct way, and how good the effect will be for our nation's life. Please see the assumption and analysis spreadsheet 5 & 6.

(6) Let 18-22 years college students enjoy "free student dormitory" and other education aid

To provide 18-22 years old Americans with free student dormitory (or in very low cost) and tuition (or in very low cost) is possible if the U.S. government can use the tax revenues in Godly wisdom. Please also see the assumption and analysis in spreadsheet 5.

How good and pleasant it is if our young generation can receive education without bearing heavy education debts, as well as can find job when they in school or after graduation.

(7) Provide part-time employee opportunity in K-12 School system for college student

To pass the education experiences, talents, knowledge from outstanding college or university students to K-12 grade children and youth will benefit all in different aspects. The college or university students can provide after school teaching aid to K-12 grade children from arts, music, sports, crafts, science, Bible to social activities etc.

The following is analysis regarding 700 billion bailout. If those funds be used in the ways to help schools and students rather than bailout banks or giants in 2008, what we can see? Please take look the analysis based on three assumptions:

---Spreadsheet-5:

IF $700 BILLION BAILOUT FUNDS IN 2008 BE USED TO OUR EDUCATION SYSTEM, WHAT CAN WE DO?	THEN, WE CAN BUILD/CREATE
Use $310 billion to Build university or college student free dormitory (at cost of 10,000 per space or apartment space) for about 31 million 18 to 24 years old young Americans in the U.S., and $390 billion for student part-time working fund.	31,000,000 units university or college student free dormitory in the U.S. for long-term use and benefits, and more
Build city kindergarten or pre-school for all children and provide burden free education system for all children, and benefit parents(at cost of 1 million cost)	700,000 city kindergarten or pre-school can be built to provide free (or at very low cost) children education system for all American families
Provide education aid fund for after school student care and activity in 98,817 U.S. public school from K-12	$7,083,801 education fund can provide for each public school

MATH CALCULATION	HOW DOES IT BENEFIT OUR EDUCATION SYSTEM?
$310,000,000,000 ÷ $10,000 = 31,000,000 units free student dormitory $390,000,000,000 ÷ 31,000,000 = $12,580 For each student part-time working fund inside campus or in public schools for K-12 education aid.	First, all 18-24 years old young Americans can receive free dormitory/apartment, and these long-term facilities can benefit students from generation to generation. Secondly, the part-time working fund $12,580 per college student can help them finish college education in debts free.
$700,000,000,000 ÷ $1,000,000 = 700,000 Kindergartens or pre-schools or daycare for 24 million U.S. little children from 0-5 years old	700,000 ÷ 35000 = about 20 kindergartens and pre-school and daycare in each U.S. city
$700,000,000,000 ÷ 98,817 = $7,083,801 (about 7 million) for each public school in the U.S. Extra education fund for K-12 after school in campus care, extended education and activities, to help parents and reduce their burdens.	Will provide extra after school part-time job opportunities to part-time teachers, university students, talents and parents to help K-12 student, provide after school free student care and let parents worry free

---Spreadsheet-6:

IF $700 BILLION BAILOUT IN 2008 BE USED TO BRING THE TEACHING OF HOLY BIBLE TO U.S. PUBLIC SCHOOL, PRISONS, AND REHABILITATION CENTER TO DO GOD'S KINGDOM WORK, WHAT CAN WE DO?	THEN, WE CAN BUILD/CREATE
Can provide new job opportunities to 10 million Bible teachers, ministers, pastors, Bible college /Seminary students to do God's kingdom education work for our nation	10 million jobs can provided with $43,750 yearly salary
Provide each American families education fund for our young generation	Each family will have $6,250 education fund
Provide 12 million unemployed people $ 58,333 education fund or financial release or working capital for starting small business.	Each person or family will have $58,333 aid either for back school education or family aid

MATH CALCULATION	HOW DOES IT BENEFIT FAMILIES & STATE?
$700,000,000,000 ÷ 10,000,000 ÷ 1.6 = $43,750 yearly salary per position (including tax and benefit)	With education of God's Word, our nation will be blessed from generation to generation, the moral standard will be raised, prisons will close one by one, rehabilitation center will become the place of praise--- and more blessings !
$700,000,000,000 ÷ 112,000,000 = $6,250 Education fund per family	Prepare saving for our young generation
$700,000,000,000 ÷ 12,000,000 = $58,333 Education fund or aid per jobless person	Help jobless person get more education or skill or repositioning

(8) **Provide a second chance to children and young people who have committed crimes or made mistakes. To care for them and their future with true love and compassion. To provide them education in the Word of God and to give every lost one a second chance and support for a new life and a fresh start. To lead them to our Creator-God and to experience God's Love and God's Saving Grace for all.**

In the past decades, taking out the Holy Bible from school system and lacking the education of Truth in the U.S. school system are the main facts which caused children or young people deviate from what is right and run away from the right path of life. The U.S. government should take this responsibility to help those lost children or adults back to right track and to get real second chance, not just let them wondering in the wildness again and again and getting worse and worse.

What the U.S. government should do is to provide them education and career training seriously, especially, work with Church system to lead those lost children or young people to the only True Living God and to let God's Love and Salvation to save their souls and bring them to right path of life. In God, everything is possible.

The assumption and analysis in spreadsheet-7 present an idea to help those who are lost and casted out from communities.

---Spreadsheet-7:

IF $700 BILLION BAILOUT IN 2008 BE USED TO PROVIDE 2ND EDUCATION CHANCE TO HELP 7.2 MILLION PEOPLE WHO ARE HELD BY JUSTICE SYSTEM (YEAR 2006'S NUMBER) TO REGAIN CONFIDENCE AND HOPE, WHAT CAN WE DO?	THEN, WE CAN BUILD/CREATE
every lost person can have $97,222 fund for 2nd chance education. The U.S. government can co-operate with Bible University or College to help them be educated in God's Word and receive true hope.	Bible college or career training center in every prison or rehabilitation center.
Create job opportunity to those people who are casted out by private business or community, to let them have fresh start to become honored citizen again.	Industries or rescue projects for lost people who are out of prison or rehabilitation center to have proper job, help them to be accepted by society again

MATH CALCULATION	HOW DOES IT BENEFIT FAMILIES & STATE?
$700,000,000,000 \div 7,200,000$ $=$ $97,222$ 2nd chance funds per lost person to attend college inside prison or rehabilitation center etc.	Turning hopeless life to full of hope and be set free in the Truth of God and free indeed, they may become missionary and serve community rather than the persons who give troubles to community.
$700,000,000,000 \div 7,200,000$ $=$ $97,222$ Funds for career and living support for each lost person	Turning the negative reality into positive through effective and active rescuing programs. It will also enhance our nation's tranquility tremendously.

In Education System, the following vital areas are worthy for Americans and U.S. leaders to think:

(1) Establishing "open to public teaching classes and testing classes" in each school district for current teachers to be re-evaluated by parents and educators--- or for those who are interesting to become teacher with teaching certificate or for those who does not have teaching certificate but have heart and desire and ability to teach in public school system with degree from University or college. To establish such evaluation system for choosing and evaluating and re-evaluating the U.S. public school's teachers will lift up and enhance the quality of the U.S. public school system.

(2) Examining union's power in education system and its effects.

(3) The true standard for evaluating teachers' qualification for young generation and America's future according to the Truth of God.

U.S. Domestic Industry & Import

Promoting and protecting U.S. domestic industry and ensuring the free capital market more free, fair and just. Promoting healthy imports and international trading to benefit Americans, our nation as well as the people worldwide.

(1) Promoting made in America domestic products

American creations, inventions and productions should be honored, promoted and inherited by Americans and U.S. government economic policies.

Setting up reasonable import tax rates, import tax rate format or structure, and the requirement of merchandise packaging and instructions are important for fair competition. All products should be clearly marked its original country rather than be marked with blurred and misleading label or instruction such as "distributed by" or "packed in the U.S.", so that, it will help and promote made in America domestic products and enhance the fair competition in free capital market.

From safety point, to mark original country in products, especially for food, is vital for protecting consumers' rights before they make choice.

(2) Boosting U.S. domestic industry

The revival for domestic industries will not only continue our nation's legacy of creation and invention, protects intellectual property rights and enhance U.S. products' competitive edges in the world, but also create new job opportunities nationwide in private business sectors.

(3) Protecting worldwide resources by setting up reasonable import tax

Setting up reasonable import tax rates based on same category domestic products' cost, its market price and consideration on nature sustainability worldwide will not only protect and promote "Made in U.S. products", but also protect and preserve worldwide environment and nature resources.

As a Christian nation, to preserve the land worldwide with good soil, good water and good air, to prevent nature abusing should be the U.S. government and corporate social responsibility.

Import tax rates and reform will be discussed in the last economy sector.

(4) Promoting imports from those countries who need help

From globe point of view, promoting import from those countries who are fall behind and poor is indirect helping hands to other nations. It will assist other nations' people to improve their living and working condition; Balancing the import and export to those nations will give them helps from two directions, and it benefits all.

(5) Healthy international trading enhances reasonable and positive resource exchange

Providing a healthy international trading environment and system will let people around the world enjoy vast nature resources God made and provided for His earthly children and meet living needs.

Setting up regulation and policies with justice and fairness are very important in order to reduce exploitation and defend foreign workers' human rights, working conditions and environments and to ensure healthy international trading and reasonable and positive resources exchange.

(6) **Promoting small businesses and encouraging people dare to dream, to create and to delight their natural talents and gifts to fulfill personal dreams, and to serve people, community and nation.**

Small and beautiful businesses not only give people opportunities to fulfill their dreams, practice their nature talents and gifts, provide good products or services to consumers, prevent depletion of resources, but also boost local employment and contribute positive strength to community and state.

To set up reasonable import tax rates and reform sales tax system are part of methods which can reduce free market's unfairness caused by monopoly, and help small businesses to survivor and to thrive.

(Tax system reform will be discussed in 10th economy sector)

(7) **Protecting "Business Legacy in Christian Faith" and preserving our nation's beauty in business sector**

The freedom of human rights should include business rights. In America, there are many Christian faith filled domestic businesses, they carry the legacy of Christianity and they are our nation's beauty and treasures. To protect and preserve our nation's beauty and treasures suppose be the U.S. government's honor and obligation. These businesses should be respected by the U.S. government.

As a nation built on the foundation of Christianity, giving freedom to such businesses to keep their religious belief in business practices should be protected by the U.S. government. They should have rights to keep their own business culture; they should have freedom to keep their religious rights in hiring, providing products and services. Their business practices according to the Word of God should be respected and protected by government.

Actually, respecting and preserving our nation's "Christian legacy in business sectors" will enhance the health in job market and free capital market if we apply the wisdom from God's Law. God's Law will always lead us to do the right things, for it is written **"God is Light, in Him there is no darkness at all"**.

Lord Jesus encourage His children: **"Be perfect, as your Heavenly Father is Perfect"**. From God's Word, we should know that "God is Perfect and God's Law is Perfect and the beauty of God's Law are beyond and surpass all men made laws and God's Law is for all human beings' eternal interests and perfection.

"God is Love", for those businesses who are truly follow God's Laws should provide right products or services, if they apply "Love" with the definition in the Holy Bible, their deeds should benefit their customers, their employees and their providers. I believe that the businesses or entities which respect the Truth of God, their business culture or practices or legacy shall benefit people, community and our nation's long-term interests.

As a Christian nation, the U.S. government should study God's Law first with humble attitude like U.S. founding fathers before formulating political polices or laws. In this way, the spiritual eyes of U.S. lawmakers and leaders will be surly opened by God's Word, and be able to know what are the real good policies for all people's ultimate and authentic benefits in the long run. It is written in Proverbs 9:10 **"The fear of the LORD is the beginning of wisdom, and knowledge of the Holy One is understanding."**

War & Homeland Security

The essential and fundamental key of victory for the war and common defense. Protecting the U.S. Army and soldiers' safety. Ensuring domestic tranquility.

(1) God's Covenant in the war of justice

As a Christian nation, a nation built upon the faith, hope and love in Lord Jesus Christ, the U.S. government and the U.S. Army have God ordained tasks as freedom defender and warrior in the world. As U.S. founding father President George Washington stated "to protect and guide all sovereigns and nations (especially such as have shown kindness to us), and to bless them with good governments, peace, and concord", the U.S. government and the U.S. Army's missions are great and honorable from God to protect freedom and justice in the world.

In order to clearly follow God's direction and accomplish His mission according to His Will, U.S. leaders as well as U.S. Military leaders need humbly seeking God and God's intervene for wars and battles before making decision. God is Justice, only the just war and battle and the side of justice will receive God's covenant and His protection.

(2) The ultimate Power and Strength for the U.S. Army is God's Covenant

From the historic events and lessons of five famous battles in the Holy Bible, we can understand that the wars or battles which under God's covenant will ultimately win, the justice speaks the final words of victory.

The five battles are good for U.S. leaders and Military leaders to read and learn: first is Abraham's battle to fight four kings and their army in Genesis Chapter 14, Abraham's 318 trained men won the battle by the power of Almighty God; second is the battle of Jericho in Joshua Chapter 5 &6, Joshua and Israelites conquered the city by obeying God's Word to march around the city seven times; the third is King David's Ziklag battle in 1 Samuel Chapter 29, the turning point's battle for King David; the fourth battle is prophet Elisha's battle with Arameans in 2 Kings Chapter 6, prophet Elisha prayed to God to open young servant's eyes to see the hills full of horses and Chariots of fire all around Elisha and won an amazing battle; fifth is the Gideon's battle in Judge Chapter 8, 300 men chosen by God Himself, followed Gideon, won the battle and defeated more than 120,000 Midianites by Almighty God's intervene.

How could these five battles win so amazingly and marvelous? The answer is that Abraham, Joshua, King David, Elisha and Gideon were all God's faithful servants who were trusting in God and obeying God's Word, they fought the battles of Justice with God's covenant, and God was with them in the battles. The Holy Bible are full of stories and events for U.S. leaders and U.S. Military leaders to study.

As a Christian nation, by obeying God's Commandments in Military,the U.S. Army will have what our father of faith Abraham had from God to keep the U.S. Army's true strength and to stand firmly as warrior and defender of Justice and freedom in the world.

For the sake of our soldiers' safety and lives, for the sake of our soldiers' families, for the sake of the entire U.S. Army, for the sake of American domestic tranquility, for the sake of America's integrity, righteousness, future and heavenly ordained missions and responsibilities to defend the freedom and peace in the world, in a Christian nation, it is very important for U.S. leaders and Military leaders to seek God, keep an intimate relationship with God, and pray to God for His Holy Presence, Intervene, Counsel, and Direction as King David did before starting or participating any war or battle and as what U.S. founding fathers did during the wars. Its importance is beyond all what we can see.

(3)   Protecting Homeland Security

Protecting Homeland Security starts from "no helping and no supporting and no training" to international political organizations or groups whose faith and belief are against the faith of Christianity, whose faith and belief are against the Most High Living God-God of Abraham, Isaac and Jacob, the Creator of the Universe. To prevent and avoid the possibility of raising up U.S. own enemies by wrong supporting action with Americans' money and resources is very important political issue for Homeland security. The U.S. leaders should stand in the Word of God to make international political policy or decision with long term vision.

The most essential focus of protecting Homeland Security in long term shall be ensuring the justice of domestic political environment. If **"Love your neighbor as yourself"** can become U.S. leaders' and lawmakers' Motto and the foundation of U.S. politic policies, **"Love never fail"** will keep our homeland in the highest degree of security and tranquility.

Whatever we do needs to follow God's Word, in this way, we will harvest the fruits of goodness.

(4) **Ensuring the U.S. Army and soldiers' safety in Military Award Programs**

To examine the operation and management security in Military **"Commercial and Government Entity"** and **"System of Award Management"** is important for protecting the U.S. Army and our soldiers. To secure those systems' safety and reliability when selecting, contracting and using products and services from private business sectors for the U.S. Army and soldiers is vital; to build up and conduct serious screens and investigations for products, services and business providers' backgrounds and identities could prevent unqualified products, services and the involvement and penetration of foreign business entities or powers or corruption forces to the U.S. Army and Military-related projects.

For examining and evaluating government contractors' qualification, to conduct "potential contractors internal employees survey and external customers survey" will be useful, practical and effective in order to choose right private business contractors and providers to provide products or services for the U.S. Army and U.S. soldiers for such honored award.

(5) **Establishing domestic people's Military Manufactories and Services to provide safe and high quality products and services to the U.S. Army and soldiers directly**

To protect the U.S. Army and soldiers thoroughly in long-term, the U.S. government should establish people's Military Industries contributed by tax revenues-people's money to provide what the U.S. Army and soldiers need. The people's Military Industries will not only ensure the U.S. Army's long term safety and security, but also boost domestic industries, and provide new job opportunities to millions.

All veterans will have no difficulty to find job and to receive their reward for their sacrifices to serve our nation.

In war and homeland security, the following issues is so important for Americans and U.S. leaders to think:

Protecting and respecting Christian Military Chaplains' praying rights in the Name of Lord Jesus Christ for our soldiers and the U.S. Army in this Christian nation.

Immigration System

Protecting U.S. immigration system's upright purposes and positive intentions. Preventing the penetration of international corruption forces in our land.

(1)   Protecting immigration law to be just and clean

The U.S. immigration law should stand in the principle of love and work for people's interests and our nation's long-term interests. In a Christian nation, this system shall be kept in just and clean.

(2)   Preventing the penetration of international illegal and corrupt money into the U.S. economy and security and domestic tranquility. Protecting and preserving our land and Americans best interests

The U.S. immigration laws should stand in justice, not to be driven by money or controlled by money, especially in the type of EB-5 business investment immigration program, the U.S. government should screen the sources of business investors' funds seriously and effectively and conduct applicants' background investigations through official cooperation with foreign governments.

To allow international corrupt money and corrupt persons flowing to America, will penetrate and endanger the U.S. economic environment, and cause Americans slowly and gradually loss land, houses, businesses, market division and buying power. The results are similar to conventional wars. It will also cause America loss its integrity and dignity to be a nation as a warrior and defender of justice in the world.

What is more, the international corrupt persons' immigration will pollute our nation's moral environment and upright spiritual condition. America, a land of faith, hope and love, should prevent to become a hiding place for international corruption forces; America should stand firmly in the Truth of God as a defender of justice to protect people's interests worldwide; the works of the U.S. government should honor God the Father, God the Son-Lord Jesus Christ, God the Holy Spirit in the front of the whole world.

In the meantime, the real estate market or land should be protected by the U.S. government for Americans' future. Setting up certain limitation or restriction for foreigners to purchase real estate or land, to check and investigate legitimacy of foreign investors' money are important for the U.S. government to think about and to take action for U.S. immigration law reform.

Elections & Lobbyists System

To free U.S. leadership from the chains of money bondage and to protect and promote the justice in the U.S. legislation system. To Encourage U.S. leaders to run the U.S. government in the purpose of serving God and people with Godly freedom.

(1) **Setting up "The U.S. Leader Election Platform"**

This is the Word of God in 2 Samuel 23:3-4
"When one rules over men in righteousness, when he rules in the fear of God, he is like the light of morning at sunrise on a cloudless morning, like the brightness after ran that brings the grass from the earth"

To elect the U.S. leaders who have hearts of righteousness and humble and love to serve God and people in this nation, to fulfill upright and clean election from federal to states and local without money wasting and money controlling, to free U.S. leaders from the chain of money bondage, to provide fair competition environment of political campaign and elections, the U.S. government should set up a nationwide "The U.S. Leader Election Platform"-a election website platform for all candidates, from various political parties to independents, to share their serving ideas with their fellows in their hometown, county, states and entire nation, and to conduct proper propagation or publicity in equal chance without paying fees.

With modern tech, to elect U.S. leaders through the form of direct and straight and simple election from federal to states to local is possible; such election will reflect all people's choices and votes more precisely. The modern tech could turn our nation's traditional election methods and plays into more fair, just, clean, effective, simple, thrifty and transparent. "The U.S. Leader Election Platform" can allow every vote matters, every vote counts, every desire and dream and voice be heard.

To design "The U.S. Leader Election Platform" as simple and very functional as possible will save whole nation's election money and energy tremendously. To design, operate and manage the project of "The U.S. Leader Election Platform" should not cost more than several million dollars yearly. It is worthy for America to try and to do for long term saving; it will let America find righteous and humble people or leaders to serve our nation; it will be the platform of politics with justice and fairness.

I hope and pray that U.S. leaders can participate political elections and serve our nation with freedom. As a Christian nation, let justice rule the U.S. elections, let U.S. leaders have courageous, brave and pure hearts to lead America to the path of Godly prosperity and blessing from generation to generation and to fulfill the calling from God for the U.S. government, fear not to the darkness forces.

(2) Setting up "Legislation Idea Contribution Platform" instead of "Lobbyists System"

The U.S. government's responsibility is serving God and people, its political policies shall be for the sake of all people; it shall not show any favor to particular interest group without just cause. So, to open the box of traditional lobbyists' system for public, the U.S. government should set up a "Legislation Idea Contribution Platform" to allow and welcome anyone or entity to speak, to present their ideas for our nation and people publicly. The valuable ideas in "Legislation Idea Contribution Platform" may give U.S. leaders and lawmakers positive help for legislation.

The modern tech can accomplish this platform in low cost to save lobbyists money and energy, to protect U.S. leaders not making unjust political decision and legislation.

The Truth of God will set U.S. leaders free and free indeed from all kinds of bondages.

Tax-1-2-3 Simplified and Transparent System

Turning the U.S. government's complicated taxes operation and management system into a simplified and transparent "Tax-1-2-3 System". To reduce the U.S. government debts and deficit. To cut and release people's and business entities' tax burdens and to reduce the U.S. government's expenditures tremendously.

Before I share ideas with you, I would like shed a little light first for the ideas I am going to share for U.S. Tax System Reform from the following simple analogy in order to make ideas easier to understand:

Analogy 1:

The U.S. government want to collect $100 tax, in first way, tax collecting cost is $80, so, the gross operating profit is $20.

The U.S. government want to collect $100 tax, in second way, tax collecting cost is $50, the gross operating profit is $50.

Obviously, in analogy 1, the second way is better than the first.

Analogy 2:

The U.S. government is going to collect $70 for government's needs and find new way to reduce the collecting cost to $15, the gross operating profit is $55.

Obviously, the analogy 2 is better than both ways in analogy 1. The tax reduced to $70, but the gross operating profit increased to $55.

The revelation from analogy 1 & 2 is that not only taxpayers' burden could be reduced from $100 to $70, but also the final gross operating profit could be increased to $55 since U.S. government tax collecting cost reduced from $80 to $50, and then from $50 to $15.

The analogy 2 shows us a hidden possibility that "reducing taxpayers' tax rates and burden", "reducing the U.S. government's operation cost", and "fulfilling the U.S. government tasks and responsibilities" could be reached and accomplished in the same time without conflict. **But, how?**

Now let me share the ideas for "**Tax-1-2-3 Simplified and Transparent System**":

Goals:

(1) Creating a simplified and transparent U.S. government tax-1-2-3 operation and management system instead of present complicated taxation system. The new tax operation and management system shall have the characters and structures of promoting and protecting honesty and fairness, easily to understand and practice, releasing tax burdens greatly from all people and business entities, and reducing the U.S. government's operation and management cost tremendously. The new system is all-win system.

(2) The U.S. government taxation system should not involve to individuals, families and businesses private activities' detail and their respective accounting system; from people to business entities, they should freely take care of and practice their own finance and activities with very limited and necessary and selected government auditing tasks in order to reduce the U.S. government huge and heavy "police-like working load" in private activities.

To free U.S. government from billions of private accounting books, give all people free space to solely manage their own finance books and be responsible on their own activities are key points for taxation system reform. Based on these points, the relationship between the U.S. government and people and businesses will be simplified, and the U.S. government expenditures will be reduced tremendously, an all win situation will be reached in America.

(3) Minimizing the U.S. government management and operation size but maximize its serving and loving function as God's servant and people's servant. As long as the U.S. government's size be reduced, all expenditures will be reduced; as long as the U.S. government system be simple and transparent, the more efficiency and effective serving function for our nation will be fulfilled.

(4) Simplifying the following tax rates with simple1-2-3 formulas and structures:

Payroll Tax, Income tax for individual and families, Income tax and sales tax for businesses (will be replaced by Business Revenue Tax in the new ideas), import tax, property tax, estate tax, inheritance tax, gift tax.

In all ideas which I am going to share, all taxes collecting formulas and structures are simplified as simple as 1-2-3, tax rates or taxes are reduced or eliminated.

As a Christian nation, America is filled with people and enterprises who have hearts of generosity to help others or community or society. The virtue and positive strength which come from people and enterprises' **free will** are more powerful and helpful than mandatory taxes.

The U.S. government should release tax burdens from people and enterprises more and more. To meet government's needs not by raising tax rates or adding type of taxes and increasing people's burdens, but by faith on a vision: if the U.S. government can strive self-discipline in government physical size and its cost in operation and management, take care of people's needs sincerely and diligently, do justly, love mercy and walk humbly with God, then, people and enterprises who have loving hearts to God, to people and our nation could positively help the U.S. government by donation. Various types of taxes and soaring rates give people pressures and burdens, but, the donation by people's free will give people joy and honor, it will please God.

(5) In America, from individuals to families, businesses, public workers and the U.S. government, from federal to state and local, we will have more time, energy, financial ability, friendly and peaceful environment to enjoy our lives with true freedom in this Christian nation, and fulfill the U.S. Constitution Dream and individual dreams.

Ideas:

1. Payroll Tax: base on wage

(1) For employee:

Employee pay: 10%

Employer pay: 10%+10%= 20%

(2) For employee who is business owner with regular payroll:

Payroll tax rate: 10%+10% for employee and employer (dual identity)

(3) For employee who is business owner without regular payroll:

Total payroll tax=yearly personal draws x (10%+10%)

(4) For business owner who does not work in company, only receive investor's dividend from profit: No payroll tax, but need to pay "personal income tax"

The payroll tax revenues, as I previously analyzed, should be used to build and create what people need for: National Medical & Health Care System, Social Security for Retirement, Poor & Poor Families, Disabled, Veterans and their families, taking care orphans and abused children and other Charity needs etc.

Once the National Medical and Health Care System finish, present "workers compensation insurance" and "group health Insurance" from private insurance providers can be replaced by new system.

Besides the National Medical & Health Care System, if private business would like to buy extra workers compensation or health insurance for employees from private insurance providers or medical providers, that should be company's sole discretion, not mandatory by the U.S. government.

2. Individual or Family Income Tax:

Base on the net income:

The net income=wages+ investment income-money for taking care of parents-donation

(1) Individuals or families who does not have child or dependent:

If net income is under $50,000: no income tax

If net income is from $50,000 to 60,000: tax rate 5%

If net income is from $60,000 to $70,000: tax rate 6%

If net income is from $70,000 to $80,000: tax rate 7%

If net income is from $80,000 to $90,000: tax rate 8%

If net income is from $90, to $100,000: tax rate 9%

If net income is $100,000 and up: tax rate 10%

(2) Individuals or families who have child or dependent:

The tax rate will be 1% deduction for each child or dependent

In this way, the U.S. government will have very simple tax return form and procedure as easy as 1-2-3.

3. Replace traditional "Business Income Tax and Sales Tax" with "Business Revenue Tax". No more Sales tax. The formulas are same for all types of businesses. The partnership, corporation, LLC and sole proprietorship etc share same formula.

Based on the net revenue and proportion of stocks:

Net revenue = total revenue-donation

Proportion of stocks between citizen owned and non-citizen owned

(1) 100% U.S. Citizen owned business: 10% x net revenue

(2) If citizen & non-citizen owned business: (10% x stock% of owned by citizen +20% x stock% of owned by non-citizen) x net revenue

(3) If non-citizen owned business: 20% x net revenue

From Tax-1-2-3, the U.S. government does not need to track private business accounting book, just simply to collect taxes base on business revenue, make tax collecting system and formula as simple as possible, and leave private accounting books as their own business and for their shareholders.

(4) If business create pollution either natural pollution or moral, that means the businesses are harmful to people's health or life or family's life or community life etc, an extra revenue tax should be added, such as 10% or more as compensation to society and community, and to be used for specific government rescuing and recovering projects or programs for victims or natural environments protection or restoration etc.

4. Import tax

To protect U.S. domestic industries, make free market more fair, promote healthy international trading, import and export to achieve worldwide resources sharing and exchanging for mutual benefits, help those nations who are fall behind and poor through healthy international trading, prevent nature resources abusing, prevent unhealthy products' penetrating in the U.S. market and polluting our land, to cut government operation and management cost and set up a simplified and transparent import tax collecting system are the key points and considering for setting up import tax formula and structure.

The following illustrations or assumptions are the ideas for import tax structure and formula:

(1) Simply set up import merchandise category in A, B, C, D, E

Category A: No U.S. domestic industry or very limited domestic production

Category B: U.S. domestic industry are strong or once strong but getting weak now

Category C: U.S. intellectual-related products or invented or initiated in the U.S.

Category D: U.S. Military or public infrastructure or safety and security related products.

Category E: Products which cause natural or moral pollution or damage, harm people health or wealth, against upright family value, endanger community environment and damage our nation's integrity and founding faith, collectively call them "Eliminated products".

(2) Setting up import tax rates base on "importer's item selling price" will make free market more fair. However, since the "importer's item selling price" are not easy to practice, an idea for "taxable value index" will be introduced as the following.

(3) Create "taxable value index" for market fairness for Category B, C, D, E:

- For small importer and wholesaler, the "taxable value index" will be:

  Taxable value index=Import invoice value x2

- For importer who are also run retail chains, the "taxable value index" will be:

  Taxable value index=Import invoice value x4

(4) Set up simple tax rates based on "taxable value index" for A, B, C, D category from 0% to 10%

Import tax= tax rate x taxable value index

Assumption:

Category A: no import tax or very low tax rate, such as 1%

Category B, C, D: tax rate from 2% to 10%.

This formula will conduce fair competition between small importers and import giants with retail chains, protect domestic industries and small retailers in the U.S.

(5) Set up penalty import tax for Category E-for "Eliminated products" as:

Import tax for Category E= (10% + penalty tax rate) x taxable value index

For those products which severely cause natural or moral pollution or damage, harm people's health or wealth, stand against upright family value, endanger community environment and damage our nation's integrity and founding faith should be prohibited to import to the U.S.

5. Property tax:

Setting up property tax formula based on the size of land and building, not on property value or price.

For example, the formula could be like this:

Property tax= A% x land size+ B% x building size

Since the size of land and building is relatively constant, it is easy to calculate, also this simple formula reflects a fact of how much resources the specific property takes in certain community.

To design reasonable rate A and B, may keep this in considering: The yearly property tax should be less than or equal to 1% of property value or price at a certain time.

6. Estate tax:

Basically, no estate tax.

Estate is a fact and reflection of love in family or between people who love and care for each other, government tax policy should respect the heritage. As long as inheritor continues to pay property tax from inherited estate, the estate tax should be eliminated, and inheritor may need to pay a reasonable transaction fee to the government instead. For example, setting up a transaction fee equals to one year property tax based on net estate.

Net estate= total estate-all debts and claims against estate-funeral expense-donation-estate transaction fee-service fee for debts and claims

Since the U.S government will involve in resolving debts, a service fee for providing such services may also be charged based on the amount of debts and its complexity. The service fee should be less than or equal to 10% of debts.

7. Inheritance tax:

Basically, no inheritance tax for states or local.

The reason for no inheritance tax is same as the estate tax, let inheritor/ beneficiaries carry on the memory of the love and care from deceased without financial obligation and burden.

Same as federal, state or local may charge reasonable transaction fees for inheritance.

8. Gift tax

The gift is also a reflection of love and care. The gifts between immediate members in families should be tax free.

9. Tax issue for new business

To encourage people to run their own business and help new business to thrive, the U.S. government should give tax and fees exempt for those whose revenue cannot cover business basic expenses, such as rent, utility.

10. Oversea U.S. business tax

To protect U.S. domestic employment environment and condition, and market sharing, those U.S. businesses who have oversea manufactory or base may need to pay extra tax contributed for the U.S. government's unemployment rescuing programs.

In Tax System and political policy, as a Christian nation, the following vital issue is worthy for U.S. leaders and law makers to think seriously:

Churches tax exemption and rights should be granted by the U.S. government without any restriction and condition related political concerns. Churches should always have rights to speak for community issues or government political issues and matters. The U.S. government should respect and treat Churches of Jesus Christ as brothers who work for God, serve God and God's Plan and God's Will in different platform.

So, in this Christian nation, the Churches of Jesus Christ should be granted the 501C (3) tax-exemption and the rights of free speech in community issues or political issues at the same time.

May the U.S. government and Churches of Jesus Christ encourage each other, help each other, and work in different platforms in harmony to serve God and all people side by side and hand in hand.

Conclusion for theme three:

"Love the Lord your God with all your heart and with all your soul and with all your strength and with all your mind and Love your neighbor as yourself" will create the pools of love and the rivers of blessing, and turn chaos to cosmos and blessing.

It is written in Micah 6:8, the word spoke from the prophet is the Word of God and the Will of God: **"He has showed you, O man, what is good and what does the LORD require of you? To act justly and to love mercy and to walk humbly with your God"**. If we do as God required, our Faith in God and the Power from God will enable our nation to **"Turning U.S. government tax revenues into the lakes of love and the rivers of blessing to benefit all people living in this beautiful and amazing land, a land of brave and freedom and dream, a land carried on the wings of Faith, Hope and Love, a nation built on the foundation of Christianity, by the Mercy, Forgiveness, Guidance, Grace and Love from Almighty God"**.

Notes in Theme III:

Social Security revenue and expenditure:
http://en.wikipedia.org/wiki/Social_Security_(United_States)

Government revenue:
http://en.wikipedia.org/wiki/United_States_federal_budget

Deficits:
http://en.wikipedia.org/wiki/Deficit_reduction_in_the_United_States

Expenditures:
http://en.wikipedia.org/wiki/
Expenditures_in_the_United_States_federal_budget
http://www.usgovernmentspending.com/breakdown

National debt of the United States:
http://en.wikipedia.org/wiki/National_debt_of_the_United_States

United State federal budget:
http://en.wikipedia.org/wiki/United_States_federal_budget

Federal Reserve:
http://en.wikipedia.org/wiki/Federal_Reserve_System

Education:
http://www.childstats.gov/americaschildren/tables/pop1.asp
http://nces.ed.gov/fastfacts/display.asp?id=98
http://www.edreform.com/2012/04/k-12-facts/

Incarceration in the United States:
From Wikipedia, the free encyclopedia

Medical and Health:
http://wiki.answers.com/Q/How_many_hospitals_in_United_States
http://www.census.gov/econ/census02/data/us/US000_62.HTM#N621
http://www.eeoc.gov/stats/jobpat/2003/naics4/6214.html
http://www.census.gov/econ/census02/data/us/US000_62.HTM#N621

Welfare:
https://www.weeklystandard.com/blogs/report-us-spent-37-trillion-welfare-over-last-5-years_764582.html

Social Program:
http://en.wikipedia.org/wiki/Social_programs_in_the_United_States

Church:
http://wiki.answers.com/QHow_many_Christian_Churches_in_the_US

Theme IV

The History Speaks

Urge the U.S. government preserve and protect our nation's most
valuable and precious heritage and legacy-The Christianity,
to do justly, to love mercy, and to walk humbly with God
the Father, God the Son-Jesus Christ, God the Holy Spirit,
and to rebuild "The Wall of the Truth" in America

1. The revelation of "Declaration of Independence"

From "Declaration of Independence", we know where America came from and what U.S. founding fathers and Americans had fought for.

The freedom America has is costly. The U.S. government and U.S. leaders should remember U.S. founding fathers' dream of freedom and Americans efforts and sacrifices for the freedom from generation to generation; learn from them and defend the Truth of God and lead our nation to the path of life-The Truth of God, and stand firmly on the Rock of Christianity.

2. The Hope from Israel's History and lessons---Rebuild "The Wall of the Truth"

Israel's history in the Holy Bible told us, when Israelites fixed their eyes on God, they were protected and blessed; when Israelites turned away from God and fixed their eyes on the world and committed sins against God, they suffered the consequences of their sins. Israel's lessons are our lessons.

As a Christian nation, the Holy Bible-the Word of God is our nation's ultimate Law. The U.S. government should learn from the faithful servant and hero and leader Nehemiah to rebuild "The Wall of the Truth" in America in this critical time, and to let the U.S. be truly protected and blessed from inside to outside by God.

3. Encouraging the U.S. government to reform and win U.S. economic battles

Only the Truth of God will set our nation free in all areas, from economic crisis to moral crisis. Lord Jesus said in Matthew 11:18 "Come to me, all you who are weary and burdened, and I will give you rest". I encourage the U.S. government to reform according to the Word of God, to seek God humbly and depends on Him, to face our nation's crises with urgency, carefully and seriously to deal with economic issues and be prepared well for the crises to come.

May Americans and U.S. leaders be more than conquerors and stand firmly in the Truth of God.

Theme V

The Hope of Fulfilling the U.S. Constitution Dream

For America, a Christian nation, only the "Faith and Hope and Love in Christ Jesus" will fulfill the U.S. Constitution Dream.

For America, a Christian nation, our only HOPE is our LORD and SAVIOR JESUS CHRIST, besides Him, there is no salvation and hope.

Urge the U.S. government and all Americans to recall and read the God's Word in Isaiah 9:6 **"For to us a Child is born, to us a Son is given, and the government will be on His shoulders. And He will be called Wonderful Counselor, Mighty God, Everlasting Father, Prince of Peace."** Let us remember our beloved Lord and Savior Jesus Christ, the KING of the Kings, the LORD of the Lords, the WORD-THE TRUTH OF GOD came to the world in flesh with humility, He came to the earth He created, He came to His people He created, He shed His Precious Blood and died on the Cross to pay all human beings death penalty to save us from our sins, because we all have sinned against God and we all short the glory of God, our sins separated us from God! He was resurrected at the third day to give all mankind the hope of eternity and the heavenward lives.

Jesus said in John 14:6 **"I am the way and the truth and the life. No one comes to the Father except through me."** Our God the Father sent His only begotten Son Jesus Christ to this lost world to Save, to Heal, to Forgive, to Love, How Great is our God! How Great our God's Love!

Our nation, a Christian nation, must listen the Word of God in 2 Chronicles 7:14 and to receive God's forgiveness and healing for our nation: **"if my people, who are called by my name, will humble themselves and pray and seek my face and turn from their wicked ways, then will I hear from heaven and will forgive their sin and will heal their land."** This is the promise from our God, as long as we keep our nation's first love-Lord and Savior Jesus Christ, be led by His Cross, be cleansed by His Precious Blood, trust in Him, love Him, depend on Him and walk with Him in all things, God will lead our nation, from individuals to families, from businesses to societies and communities, from state government to federal government, walk out from the spiritual darkness and confusion, and walk out from all kinds of crises.

Behold America, our Lord Jesus Christ will come back soon. Let us be prepared for the Lord's second coming; let us run the race for God and let our nation truly become **"The salt of the earth, the light of the world"** (Matthew 5:13, 14), a true champion nation and more than conqueror in the world, a true defender for the Truth, a true warrior for the freedom and peace in the whole world.

Our Lord and Savior Jesus said in John 8:12 **"I am the light of the world. Whoever follows me will never walk in darkness, but will have the light of life."**, let our nation walk into God's great Light and shine like stars in the universe in this crooked and depraved generation, let us walk in the God's promises and give God thanks and praise and worship for His greatest Amazing Love and Amazing Grace: **"For God so loved the world that He gave His one and only Son, that whoever believes in Him shall not perish but have eternal life." (John 3:16)**

God's Word is my life, God's smile is my heaven. I pray and hope for this nation to live in God's Word and see His smile from heaven. **GOD IS LOVE!** In **Luke 15:11-32**, Lord Jesus tells us an amazing story of a prodigal son and his Father, **this is the parable for our nation's hope.**

"Let us fix our eyes on Jesus, the author and perfecter of our faith" (Hebrews 12:2), let us never forget what God has done for us, remember all His goodness and give Him thanks and praise and worship; let us receive His Saving Grace-the Salvation of the Cross, and pray for our lives, our families, Churches of Jesus Christ, the U.S. government and leaders, our nation's future and the whole world **in Jesus Holy Name:**

"Our Father in heaven, hallowed be Your name,
Your kingdom come, Your will be done
on earth as it is in heaven.
Give us today our daily bread.
Forgive us our debts,
as we also have forgiven our debtors.
And lead us not into temptation,
but deliver us from the evil one.
For Yours is the Kingdom and the Power and the Glory forever,
Amen!" (Matthew 6:9-13)

It's time to take action

Economy is the essential foundation in a nation

A real strong and healthy economic system must be a system established on the foundation of the Truth of God. From individual to family, from business to nation, we need God's Word to guide our path.

History gives lessons. We must listen and learn.

If the roots of economy are strong and healthy, its fruits will be good.

The 2008 economic crisis is an alarm, it urges us that our nation needs take serious action to reform U.S. economic system.

A corrupt economic system will absolutely lead a nation to be left behind or fall behind and to be defeated in the world. The histories in the world gives us lessons and wake up calls.

In order to confront new era's economic challenges and to overcome future crises, the U.S. government and Americans need to be ready and be equipped well.

It's time for the U.S. government to examine and reform U.S. political and economic system according to the Truth of God for the sake of people and our nation's future. It's time to take action for system operation to pull out sick and poisoned roots. The 2008 economic crisis is not over, it still threaten us and weaken our nation's economic system and economic strength.

Be Strong and Courageous to stand in the Truth, only the Truth can ensure U.S economy strong and healthy, only the Truth can set our nation free and free indeed!

Let's climb to the Peak of the Mountain

One day,

I heard the song, a song flying from the Peak of the Mountain

in sweet melody

"I want this little bird to fly, I want this little bird to fly---"

Oh, I know, it came from heaven, my home.

In the echo, I sung back:

"I long to fly to Your Loving Arms, the Vast Blue Sky"

Yes, like a little bird, I sing and fly,

"If I rise on the wings of the dawn, if I settle on the far side of the sea,

even there Your hand will guide me,

Your right hand will hold me fast"

I sing, I dance, I run, I climb, to the Peak of the Mountain,

with new song and dream and hope, I run, I climb---

Oh, my friends, my brothers and sisters,

children of the Most High Living God,

Let's climb together to the Peak of the Mountain,

up there,

we will be embraced by the hope and joy

and peace and beautiful scenery!

Oh, heaven, my sweet home---

Let's climb together to the Peak of the Mountain!

Notes

Notes for Theme I:

The United States Constitution

Christianity and the Constitution-the Faith of Our Founding Fathers
Author:
John Eidsmoe, Published by Baker Book House Company,
www.bakeracademic.com

Notes in Theme III:

Social Security revenue and expenditure:
http://en.wikipedia.org/wiki/Social_Security_(United_States)

Government revenue:
http://en.wikipedia.org/wiki/United_States_federal_budget

Deficits:
http://en.wikipedia.org/wiki/Deficit_reduction_in_the_United_States

Expenditures:
http://en.wikipedia.org/wiki/Expenditures_in_the_United_States_federal_budget
http://www.usgovernmentspending.com/breakdown

National debt of the United States:
http://en.wikipedia.org/wiki/National_debt_of_the_United_States

United State federal budget:
http://en.wikipedia.org/wiki/United_States_federal_budget

Federal Reserve:
http://en.wikipedia.org/wiki/Federal_Reserve_System

Education:

http://www.childstats.gov/americaschildren/tables/pop1.asp
http://nces.ed.gov/fastfacts/display.asp?id=98
http://www.edreform.com/2012/04/k-12-facts/

Incarceration in the United States:

From Wikipedia, the free encyclopedia

Medical and Health:

http://wiki.answers.com/Q/How_many_hospitals_in_United_States
http://www.census.gov/econ/census02/data/us/US000_62.HTM#N621
http://www.eeoc.gov/stats/jobpat/2003/naics4/6214.html
http://www.census.gov/econ/census02/data/us/US000_62.HTM#N621

Welfare:

https://www.weeklystandard.com/blogs/report-us-spent-37-trillion-welfare-over-last-5-years_764582.html

Social Program:

http://en.wikipedia.org/wiki/Social_programs_in_the_United_States

Church:

http://wiki.answers.com/Q/How_many_Christian_Churches_in_the_US

About the Author:

Ling Ling Shi, a Chinese American, a Christian, came to the U.S. in 1988. She has worked as an engineering teacher, accountant, insurance agent, importer, retailer, newspaper publisher, commercial producer & director, TV program director, song writer and screenplay writer etc. She is the author of the book "Build An American ARK-the Strategy and Method for U.S. Economic Revival".

www.ingramcontent.com/pod-product-compliance
Lightning Source LLC
Chambersburg PA
CBHW030903180526
45163CB00004B/1690